D1712621

TAKING ACTION AGAINST

Taking Action

Family Breakups

Sarah Levete

rosen publishing's
rosen central

New York

Jefferson Twp. Public Library
1031 Weldon Road
Oak Ridge, NJ 07438
973-208-6244
www.jeffersonlibrary.net

Published in 2010 by The Rosen Publishing Group Inc.
29 East 21st Street, New York, NY 10010

Copyright © 2010 Wayland/The Rosen Publishing Group, Inc.

All rights reserved. No part of this book may be reproduced
in any form without permission from the publisher, except
by a reviewer.

First Edition

Editors: Sarah Eason and Robyn Hardyman
Editor for Wayland: Katie Powell
Consultant: Jayne Wright
Designers: Paul Myerscough and Rob Norridge
Picture researcher: Maria Joannou

Library of Congress Cataloging-in-Publication Data

Levete, Sarah.
  Taking action against family breakups / Sarah Levete.
      p. cm. -- (Taking action)
  Includes index.
  ISBN 978-1-61532-310-4 (library binding)
  ISBN 978-1-61532-311-1 (paperback)
  ISBN 978-1-61532-312-8 (6-pack)
  1. Single parent families--Juvenile literature.
  2. Broken homes--Juvenile literature. 3. Families--Juvenile
  literature. I. Title.
  HQ759.915.L479 2010
  306.89--dc22
                          2009027028

Photo Credits:
Cover photographs: Shutterstock/Suzan (top), Corbis/Rick Gomez (bottom).
Interior photographs: Alamy Images: Catchlight Visual Services 6, Angela
Hampton Picture Library 33; Corbis: Creasource 20, Rahat Dar/EPA 30–31;
Fotolia: Duane Ellison 10, TheFinalMiracle 5; Getty Images: Stone/Kevin
Cooley 40; Istockphoto: Bobbieo 11, Robert Churchill 22, Digitalskillet 9,
Fotocromo 32, Sergey Lagutin 24, Andrea Laurita 45, Nikolay Mamluke 4,
Juan Monino 21, Vikram Raghuvanshi 8, Barbara Sauder 37, TommL 27;
Rex Features: Giuliano Bevilacqua 16–17, c.W. Disney/Everett 39, Ken Katz
42, Most Wanted 29; Shutterstock: Galina Barskaya 15, 43, Andi Berger 28,
Bronwyn Photo 41, David Davis 12, Jaimie Duplass 2–3, Mandy Godbehear
13, Anthony Harris 38, David Hughes 34, Iofoto 18, Tan Kian Khoon 36,
Losevsky Pavel 35, Kristian Sekulic 19, Raluca Teodorescu 1, 14, Paolo
Vairo 25, Tracy Whiteside 44; Wayland Archive: 47.

Manufactured in China
CPSIA Compliance Information: Batch #WAW0102YA: For Further Information
contact Rosen Publishing, New York, New York at 1-800-237-9932

CONTENTS

Chapter 1

What is family breakup?

Do you live with two parents, one parent, guardians, or grandparents? Your parents may be living together or living separately. Adult relationships between couples, whether or not they are married, sometimes break down. A breakup is hard for everyone involved, but it is especially difficult when either adult has children—either their own children or children for whom they are responsible. Family breakup affects many children and young people every year.

Breaking up

If a couple decides to separate, their children have to live apart from one parent. Children from a family whose parents have separated or split up are often said to come from a "broken home."

There are many terms to describe a family after a breakup. These include a lone-parent, single-parent, and one-parent family. These terms can also refer to a family where a parent has died, or where only one parent has ever lived with the children. Are these terms accurate? In many cases, both parents remain involved in the care of their children, even if one parent has most of the day-to-day responsibility.

You may be very upset if your parents split up, but in the long run, it might be easier than hearing arguments all the time.

Family breakup is difficult for people of any age. It can be particularly hard for young people, who are beginning to become more independent but who still need the security of their family.

Divorce or separation

Some parents are married; other parents live together. A married couple who separate usually get a divorce. This marks the legal end of the marriage, after which each partner will be able to marry again. A couple who live together do not need to get a divorce, although they might still seek legal advice about which of them will take care of their children.

What's the big deal about family?

Home should be the place where you feel safe and secure, and unconditionally loved—whatever happens. It's where you can let go of your worries about friendships or school, or share those worries with your parents. Although parents and brothers and sisters can be irritating, they are also often the people who give you love and support. So when parents separate, it can feel as if the safety net and comfort zone of home and family has been ripped apart.

FACTS

✳ **9% of families in the United States are single-parent families.**

✳ **20% of families in the United Kingdom are single-parent families.**

✳ **14% of families in Australia are single-parent families.**

Different families

The way in which children find out about a breakup varies. Some parents separate gradually over time, but they make other living arrangements. Others split very quickly.

Families come in many shapes and sizes. Some have several children, others only one. Many families begin with two parents or a couple living together as the carers of the children. One or both adults may be the biological parents, or the children may be adopted or fostered, or be stepchildren. Some parents are in homosexual relationships—they are called same-sex parents. Any type of family can experience a breakup.

It happened to me

"I've always lived with my dad and his partner, John. When they split up, it was horrible. I stayed with dad but missed John loads. Kids at school were really unkind—they didn't think that I came from a 'real family,' so they didn't see why I was upset. I still see John sometimes, which is good."

Aimee, age 12.

TALK ABOUT

According to the *United Nations Convention on the Rights of Children, 1989*:

"… the child, for the full and harmonious development of his or her personality, should grow up in a family environment, in an atmosphere of happiness, love, and understanding."

Consider these questions about the family environment:

✳ What do you think makes a family?

✳ Do you think families are important—why?

✳ Do you think it is better for children to live with two parents or with one, and why?

How and when does a breakup happen?

A family can break up at any time, when a baby is young or when the children have grown up and are living independently. Whenever it happens, and whatever the makeup of the family, a breakup creates many complex feelings and inevitably involves change for all the individuals involved.

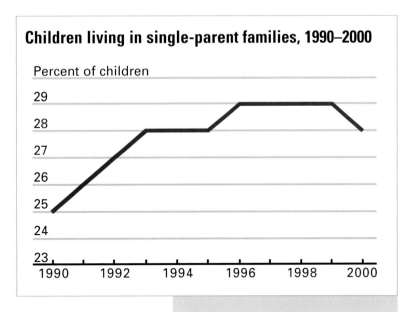

Children living in single-parent families, 1990–2000

This graph shows the percentage of children in the United States living in single-parent families, from 1990 to 2000.

Some children are aware of difficulties between their parents and may not be surprised when they split up, but for others, it can be a total shock. Sometimes, one parent leaves very suddenly; in other families, both parents stay in the house while arrangements are made. However a breakup happens, every family deals with the separation in its own unique way.

Chapter 2

Why do families break up?

Every family has its ups and downs, with arguments, upsets, and tensions. But when these become overwhelming, some couples decide there is no future for them together and that they are better off apart. The reasons why a couple separates are unique to them, just as their relationship is unique.

Falling out of love

Sometimes a couple who have been content with each other simply fall out of love. They may begin to treat each other more like housemates or friends rather than loving partners, and find that they don't share any interests, except for their children. Some couples are content to continue in this way but others are not. There is no right or wrong.

One person may unexpectedly meet someone else, fall in love with them, and start an affair. The new relationship may last or it may end—but an affair is often the cause of a family breakup.

Arguments

Everyone argues. Arguments can be about money worries, health problems, work troubles, or over simple things, such as who washes the dishes. Arguments and disagreements can be healthy ways of expressing feelings and finding solutions to difficulties in a relationship, but when they become the main way of communicating, a couple may decide it is better to separate.

All relationships have ups and downs, but when a couple is unhappy together most of the time, separation may be the best option.

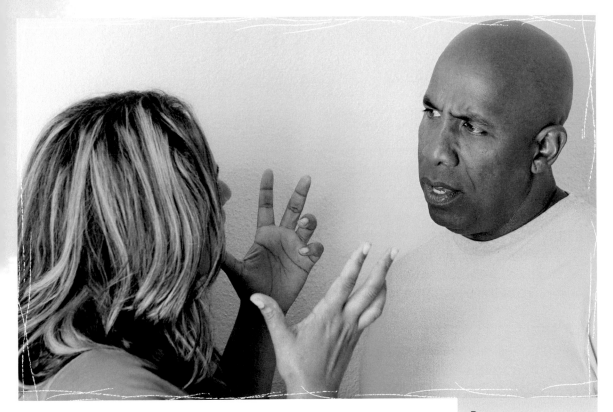

It's not your fault

Parents often argue about their children—perhaps about how to discipline a young person, or when a child's bedtime should be. You might be concerned that your behavior has caused rifts between your parents. It may contribute to their arguments, but this doesn't cause a relationship to break down completely. Parents decide to separate because of problems in their relationship as a couple, and not because of any difficulties they might have with their children.

Parents may argue about all kinds of things, from money to who does the household chores.

It happened to me

"Me and my sister always argued and fought. We irritated each other about everything. Mom and Dad got really angry with us. Then they'd get angry with each other and argue about how to deal with us. When Dad told us he was moving out, I blamed myself—and my sister. But Mom told me recently it was because she had met someone else and didn't love Dad any more."

Ali, age 11.

Harmful relationships

Although a breakup is often caused by the feelings one partner has, or doesn't have, for the other, it can also be caused by one partner's aggressive or unpredictable behavior. Some adult relationships are abusive—one partner regularly abuses or physically harms the other partner. Such behavior is unacceptable. A partner in this situation may decide to leave, although this may not always be the easy thing to do.

Domestic abuse is when a parent or partner hits, intimidates, or bullies anyone in the home. Abuse isn't always physical; it is also repeatedly saying threatening things or making a person feel very bad about him or herself. A person who suffers domestic abuse may be too frightened to do anything—even to leave. If you are in this situation, talk to an adult you trust or contact one of the organizations that offer confidential support and advice for both adults and children (see page 47).

A problem with alcohol can put great pressure on a family and the relationships within it.

Coping with addiction

Alcohol and drugs can change a person's behavior. Someone who is often drunk or high on drugs may say or do things that he or she wouldn't usually do. They may become violent and abusive. However guilty the person feels afterward, or however much he or she may promise that it won't happen again, the behavior is hurtful, frightening, and can even sometimes be very dangerous for the rest of the family.

Coping with a partner's addiction or difficulty with drinking or drugs puts a huge strain on the relationship. The partner may not feel able to remain in the relationship. It is unlikely that the addict's behavior will change until he or she has overcome the addiction.

Why can't they stay together?

Have you ever stayed at a friend's house and seen their parents arguing, and wondered how they can still stay together? If your parents have recently separated, you might feel confused about why they couldn't have dealt with their difficulties and stayed together. Different people make different decisions and have their own issues to deal with—comparing your situation with someone else's won't help your family's situation.

No one should feel unsafe or threatened at home. Violence and abuse are unacceptable, whether toward a partner or children within the family.

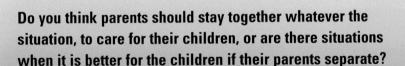

Do you think parents should stay together whatever the situation, to care for their children, or are there situations when it is better for the children if their parents separate?

Chapter 3

How do people feel in a family breakup?

Angry, upset, lonely, scared, glad, relieved, shocked? There are many emotions a young person goes through when his or her family breaks up—sometimes all at once. It can feel like being on an emotional roller-coaster, with no way to get off. Change will happen; things will be different. Overnight, what a person felt secure about may be uprooted. Accepting, understanding, and getting used to the changes—which may well be unpredictable—takes time.

But it's their job!

Parents should nurture and love their children from the moment they are born, or as soon as they begin to take care of them. That's the job of being a parent. It can seem as if parents give up that job when they separate. Children and young people are usually the main focus of parents' attention. During a breakup, they may suddenly feel they are not important any more— if they were, would their parents have split up?

If you feel angry about your parents' breakup, it is better to talk to them about it rather than hide your feelings.

All young people need a lot of reassurance, support, and attention at a time when parents are often preoccupied, worried, and unhappy. Family breakup can make young people unsure of where they belong, both in a practical sense of where to live and in an emotional sense.

A young person may feel betrayed by the very people who are supposed to provide security and love. Feelings of anger, hurt, and even hatred are often common. But it's important to realize that parents, too, deserve healthy, loving relationships; and it usually makes them better and happier parents, too.

Everyone reacts differently to a family breakup. Some people may feel glad that the arguments are over, but others may feel very sad that their parents are no longer together.

Relieved or responsible

Some people feel relief when their unhappy parents separate. If life has been a pattern of arguments and unhappiness, it can be better when the fights stop. Feeling glad or relieved is not wrong—it's quite natural.

It's also common to feel responsible for the situation, even guilty. Perhaps you wanted your parents to split up; perhaps you even behaved badly to create more arguments and tension, and they did split, but now you feel guilty. It's important to remember that the breakdown of an adult relationship is just that— a decision taken by the adults alone. A breakup is never the responsibility of a child.

TALK ABOUT

✳ **Is there a right way and wrong way for children to feel when their parents split up?**

✳ **Do you think children should tell their parents how they feel, or is it better not to say anything?**

Lonely

One parent moving out can leave a huge gap in a young person's life and they can feel very lonely. Everyday things, such as not saying goodnight, or not telling a parent about a funny event that happened at school, can highlight these feelings of loneliness. Missing a parent is hard. If you argue with the parent you live with, you may just want support from your other parent—and feel sad if it is not immediately possible. Sometimes brothers and sisters have to live apart from each other when parents separate, which can add to the feelings of loneliness. Try to talk to friends or other family members about how you feel since it can make you feel less alone.

Young people often feel very confused and alone when parents separate.

Full of hope

Some young people cling to the hope that their parents will get back together. They may try to behave exceptionally well, and be extra helpful, hoping that will help their parents to repair their relationship. Or they may deliberately express extremes of unhappiness, to put pressure on their parents to "make everything OK again." But the parents have made an independent decision—their children's behavior didn't cause it, and it won't change it. It is better to concentrate on ways to accept the changes and to move on.

Blame

It's easy to blame one parent for a family breakup, particularly if it seems as if one person's behavior has been the trigger for the separation, or if one parent has left suddenly. However, there are usually lots of things that influence the parents' relationship that children are unaware of. Very few partners in a breakup can be placed neatly into the roles of the good and the bad.

It happened to me

"I hated my mom so much. I blamed her for Dad going. All I wanted to do was see Dad. I did everything possible to make things worse for Mom. I wouldn't help at home and I was rude. Then Dad talked to me—he made me realize it wasn't Mom's fault. They had both come to the decision."

Philip, age 12.

Perfect parent?

When you stay at home with one parent, he or she still has to ask you to clean up, get ready for school, or finish your homework. These everyday things often get on children's nerves and cause arguments. The absent parent isn't there to remind you it's your turn to do the dishes or to say no to your favorite TV program, so it's easy to idealize him or her and remember only the good points. It may seem as if he or she is more fun than the parent you live with, but try to be aware of the challenges that each parent faces.

Brothers and sisters

Sometimes, brothers and sisters can support each other when parents split up. After all, they understand the situation better than anyone. At other times, brothers and sisters may take sides with different parents. This can cause more tension and arguments in a period of stress and uncertainty for everyone. Younger children often turn to older ones for comfort; even if you don't feel like supporting anyone else, showing affection to confused brothers or sisters will make a big difference to them.

Brothers and sisters can offer support to each other in times of family breakup.

Unhappy parents

As you are adjusting to the changes in your family, so, too, are your parents. One or both of them may be really miserable, and it may seem as if they are not there to support you. They may even turn to you for advice, reassurance, and a shoulder to cry on. If this is the case, it's important that you have an outlet for your own feelings. Talk to other family members, to a trusted teacher, or a good friend.

It's common for one parent to be more unhappy than the other, especially if he or she didn't want to split up. Parents may feel very angry with each other. Phone calls and meetings may be tearful, angry, loud, and resentful. It's important for children to try to establish their own relationships with both parents in the new situation, regardless of how the adults behave toward each other.

Michael Phelps started swimming as a child to help him deal with his family breakup.

A child may feel great sympathy and concern for one parent, especially if he or she wanted to keep the family together. In this case, the child is dealing not only with the departure of one parent, but also with the unhappiness of the one left behind.

Weapons in a battle

Sometimes parents use children as weapons in their battle with each other. This is unfair on the children. If you think your parents are using you as a go-between to take messages from one to the other, or that one constantly criticizes the other in front of you, try to speak out about it. Ask them not to involve you in that way. Speaking clearly, calmly, and directly about this may help them to realize the damaging effect of their behavior.

It's not getting better

"Everyone will be happier," or "We'll all get along better" are the kind of reassuring words parents use when explaining a separation. This can be very hard to accept when no one does seem to be happier—in fact, everyone appears to be very unhappy. Even though parents have made the decision to part, it can take a while for them to accept that their relationship as a couple is at an end—and there may be great sadness and loneliness for both for quite a while. It takes time for everyone to get used to the new situation, even for the people who are responsible for making the decision to break up.

In the media

The U.S. swimmer, Michael Phelps, has won more Olympic Gold Medals than any other individual. He started swimming when he was seven years old to avoid the arguments between his parents, who were splitting up at the time. Phelps felt that swimming helped him to forget about his family problems for a while and reduced the stress he felt. All family breakups are stressful. It helps to find a safe and supportive way to express your feelings and let off steam. Not everyone is going to become an Olympic champion, but even just talking to a school counselor, a relative, or a friend can help—as can a good game of football or swimming.

Not the children's responsibility

However upsetting it is to see a parent unhappy or angry about the situation, it's not up to the children to make everything better. Young people can, of course, help more around the house and be sensitive to a parent's feelings and needs, but it's not their responsibility to make their parents happy. If you are concerned about a parent's well-being, talk to a trusted relative or school counselor.

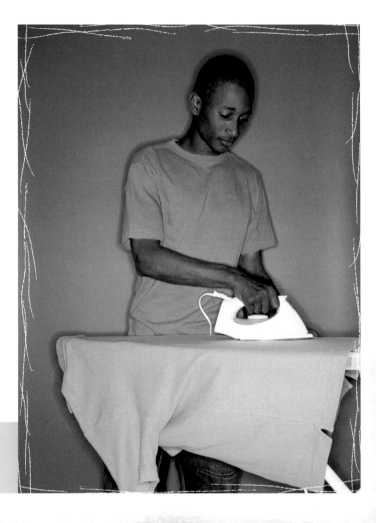

It will help your parent if you help around the house, but you can't solve all your parent's problems.

DOs & DON'Ts

✳ **Do talk about how you feel to friends, family members, or trusted teachers at school.**

✳ **Don't forget to keep pursuing activities and interests that make you feel good.**

✳ **Do write in a journal or diary, or draw about how you feel. Expressing your emotions helps to make them seem less overwhelming.**

✳ **Do tell your parents how you feel.**

✳ **Don't assume that everyone will feel the same about the breakup—not everyone will react in the same way. Some people may be relieved, others may be devastated.**

18

Speak up

Just because your parents are unhappy or preoccupied with sorting out new family arrangements, this doesn't mean that they don't have time to talk to you. You don't need to protect them from your feelings, and it's important to speak up about how you feel.

Talking doesn't repair the situation, but it helps you to deal with your feelings. Friends who have been through a similar situation are great to talk to, because they'll probably be able to identify with lots of your feelings. Talk to grandparents, uncles, and aunts, too, but ask them not to take sides. Talking about your feelings is talking about you— it's not about your parents, and it's not the time for other people to criticize either of your parents.

It is good to tell a friend how you feel.

Chapter 4

What happens when a family breaks up?

When a family breaks up, everyone is trying to deal with confused and chaotic feelings. To make matters worse, there are lots of practical things to consider and lots of changes to get used to. For some families, things change overnight and for others, it takes a while before changes are made.

Who lives with who?

The first questions most children ask are: "Which parent will I live with?" and "Where will we live?" Parents may choose to agree this between themselves or else a judge in a court makes the decision (see pages 28–29). Most often, children stay with their mother. Some parents choose joint custody where a child lives part of the week with one parent and the rest of the week with the other. Siblings usually stay together, although sometimes one child decides (and is able) to live with one parent, and their brother or sister lives with the other parent.

There are sometimes reasons why a child must stay with one particular parent. It may be to do with their safety, or their parent's ability to care for them. If parents cannot agree between themselves, the arrangements are agreed in a family court. In the case of older children, the court will take their opinions into account when making their decision. The person who takes care of the children is said to have custody of them.

Ideally, parents should agree between them who has custody of their children. But sometimes the only way an agreement can be reached is with the help of a family court.

Fostering

If neither parent is able to care for a child for a while, it may be necessary for that child to stay with relatives or to be fostered. Fostering means that another family looks after the child for a while. Being moved away from both parents can make a child feel even more insecure and worried. However, fostering also provides a stable home where a child can feel safe and secure while parents work through their difficulties. Whatever your feelings, it helps to share them with an adult, such as a teacher or social worker.

Children sometimes stay with a relative such as a grandparent while their parents sort out the new living arrangements.

DOs & DON'Ts

There are some things about your new situation that you can influence, and others that you cannot.

✳ Do tell a responsible adult clearly what you would prefer.

✳ Do accept that some decisions have to be made even if you are unhappy about them. Try to understand the reasons why those decisions have been made.

✳ Don't stay quiet if you feel unsafe staying with one of your parents—tell another trusted adult.

Moving to a new house and school

Sometimes children stay in the same house after a breakup. However, when a parent leaves the home, they may need to pay for a new home of their own. They may also pay for the home their children still live in. This can be very expensive, so children may need to leave the family home and move to a less-expensive home. A family may also move if one parent moves in with another partner.

If you move to a different area, you may well change school, too. This is another big change, but it is also an opportunity to meet new friends. You can still stay in touch with your old friends.

It can sometimes feel as if you have no choice in all this, and there are some things you can't change. But this does not mean you can't make your feelings known and express your views. The living arrangements are usually based on who is in the best position to care for the children and offer them the security they need at this time of great change and upset.

It takes time to settle into a new area and school, but sometimes such moves are unavoidable when parents split up.

Seeing both parents

TALK ABOUT

Just because a parent moves out, it doesn't mean an end to the child's relationship with that parent. Arrangements are often made so that children remain in regular contact with the absent parent. This isn't always easy or straightforward—if one parent moves a long way away, it may not always be possible to see him or her every week. If one parent is finding it difficult to adjust to the new setup, they may need some time before they can see the children on a regular basis. Always ask parents to be very clear about the arrangements for seeing the other parent.

* Do you think children should be allowed to choose whom they live with after a breakup?
* Do you think parents should only make contact arrangements if a child approves of them?
* Should parents be legally obliged to remain in contact with their children?

No contact

In some cases, a child loses all contact with the absent parent. This is in no way the child's fault; it is the adult's responsibility to keep up the contact. Sometimes, one parent might feel that the child is better off without contact; perhaps the parent is experiencing difficulties or has problems that make it too hard to remain in contact. If the contact stops, a child can feel rejected and sad. In this situation, try to focus instead on the people who are able to support you.

It happened to me

"My mom moved out and stayed with a friend. Then she got a new apartment and Dad couldn't afford the rent on our home. So we had to move. It wasn't far away, but I was fed up with having a smaller room and no yard to play ball. After about a year, things changed again and we moved to a different place. I'm still near my friends and still have a small room, but at least the atmosphere is better now, and I see Mom every weekend."

Ravi, age 12.

Chapter 5

People's attitudes to family breakup

In recent decades, society's attitudes to families, and family breakup, have changed. Fifty years ago, it was unusual for a couple to live together without being married. Since the 1960s, this has become more common, with fewer couples getting married. It has become easier to get a divorce in many countries, so the number of divorces has increased. Over the last few years, however, in the United States, there has been a drop in the number of divorces; fewer people are marrying in the first place.

Many negative stereotypes still exist for children from one-parent families. Family breakups are still often blamed for any bad behavior by young people.

It happened to me

"When my dad left, it was upsetting, but me and my sister were OK and Mom was great. But when I got into a little trouble at school, everyone seemed to think it was because my dad wasn't around. It really annoyed me that people seemed to think Mom couldn't manage on her own and it was her fault. It wasn't easy, but we were OK. The trouble at school was down to me—I got mixed up with a bad crowd, but Mom soon straightened me out!"

Leon, age 14.

TALK ABOUT

Do you agree with the statements below?

✱ Every child benefits from living with two parents.

✱ There are more pressures on a parent who brings up children alone.

✱ Family breakups are responsible for children doing badly at school, and for negative behavior in young people.

Stereotypes

It is likely that you either know people whose parents have split up or that your parents have split up. However, just as one-parent families have become more common, so prejudices have developed about the effects of this on children. Disruptive and troubled young people can sometimes come from broken homes. Some people think that coming from a one-parent family can increase a young person's chances of getting into trouble. Parts of the media even suggest that the majority of teenage troublemakers come from one- parent families. However, there are many factors that influence a young person's behavior and all the difficulties they may experience can not be blamed on the parents alone.

Barack Obama is a positive role model, yet he is from an unconventional family background. He was brought up by his mother and then his grandmother. The media don't talk about unconventional one-parent households as much as they dwell on negative role models coming from broken homes.

President Barack Obama is an example of someone who has come from a "broken home" and has gone on to become extremely successful.

Religion and divorce

In many religions, the bond of marriage is sacred and they believe divorce breaks this sacred bond. Different religions have very different attitudes toward divorce.

Within the Christian religion, Roman Catholics believe that marriage is a sacrament, a special bond and blessing witnessed by God. For this reason, there are restrictions on obtaining a divorce and a divorced person is not allowed to take part in some key religious ceremonies. The Protestant Church of England allows divorce, but only permits remarriage in a church in certain circumstances.

The Hindu religion does not allow divorce, but in some countries, Hindus still divorce anyway. If a Hindu couple do divorce, there may be a prejudice or stigma against them, particularly the woman.

Muslims accept that divorce may be necessary. Different Muslim cultures and communities have varying ideas about divorce. Some accept that a man can divorce his wife by repeating the phrase "talaq, talaq, talaq." Others do not recognize this as the formal ending of the marriage and believe that there should be periods of separation and attempts at reconciliation before a divorce.

Sikhs expect that a couple will stay married, but accept that separation and divorce are sometimes unavoidable. In Judaism, the Jewish religion, divorce is also recognized as an inevitable end to some relationships.

Changing values

Today, many people are not influenced by religious beliefs; they may decide not to marry but to live with a partner. Married or not married, the effect and upset of family breakup is still the same.

FACTS

In a recent survey, the National Center for Policy Analysis reported that in the United States:

✳ Nationally, there were about 4.2 divorces for every thousand people

✳ The rate was 8.5 per thousand in Nevada, 6.4 in Tennessee, 6.1 in Arkansas and Oklahoma.

✳ Of the southeastern states, only South Carolina's rate of 3.8 was below the national average.

Attempts to reduce the divorce rate include:

✳ Pre-marital counseling

✳ Values and relationship teaching in public schools

✳ Couples encouraged to accept mediation before deciding to divorce.

TALK ABOUT

Most couples, whatever their religious beliefs, enter marriage believing it to be a union for life.

* Do you think that the increasing number of couples choosing not to marry reflects a reduction in the influence of religious values?

* Does religion make any difference to people today when they think about families?

Chapter 6

The law and family breakup

The media often features wealthy celebrities fighting in a divorce court over their money, property, and children. Many couples decide on their family arrangements between themselves, but some ask for legal help to reach agreements over the custody of their children and the financial arrangements for supporting them.

Supporting the children

All married couples are bound by a legal agreement. If they separate, they usually end the marriage legally—by getting divorced. A judge decides whether or not to grant the divorce, and the couple don't always need to be present when this happens. An unmarried couple do not need to get a divorce, but they must decide who will take care of the children and how much money the other parent will pay toward this care, called child support.

Money is often a source of conflict between parents when they break up. In some countries, the parent who does not live with the children is still legally obliged to contribute money for the things they need, such as food and clothes. Sometimes parents argue about the amount this parent pays, and this can lead to tensions.

In most cases, the mother has custody of the children from a relationship. This is because in the past, it was usually the mother who stayed at home to take care of them. In the United States, some fathers campaign for better rights to see their children, and for different systems to decide how much money they should to pay to support them.

Whomever the children live with, their other parent will usually have rights to see them regularly.

Family breakups are difficult for all children, but they are especially hard for children who are in the public eye.

In the media

Pop star Britney Spears is the mother of two young children. She and her ex-husband, Kevin Federine, separated, and in full glare of the media, they fought over the custody of their children. Spears is said to have begun to take drugs, and as her behavior became erratic and unpredictable, the courts gave custody of the children to her ex-husband. Spears now has visiting rights to see her children. Most family breakups do not happen in such a public way and with such drama, but any family breakup is very stressful and upsetting, especially for young people.

Mediation

Many couples try to avoid upsetting battles over children and money in court. Instead, they ask for legal support when they are breaking up, to make the separation as easy as possible, especially for the children. This support is called mediation. A trained counselor, called a mediator, discusses with the parents how to make their separation less traumatic.

29

Different countries, different laws

Every country has its own laws about when and how people can divorce. For example, in Japan, in some circumstances a couple can divorce by simply signing a formal paper in front of two witnesses. The Philippines, a Catholic country, does not allow divorce. Each country also has its own laws relating to custody. This can cause great confusion, complication, and upset if a family breaks up and the each parent wants to live, with their children, in different countries.

With international travel now so easy, many more people have relationships with people from different countries and cultures. If these relationships then break down, there may be disputes about which country the children should live in, particularly if one parent returns to his or her home country after the breakup.

In the
media

Molly Campbell was a 12-year-old girl, also known as Misbah Rana, who used to live with both her parents in Scotland. In 2006, after her parents separated, her father took her to live in Pakistan, against her mother's wishes. There was a great deal of speculation in the media about whether or not Molly/Misbah had been taken against her will. Molly/Misbah currently lives with her father and sisters in Pakistan.

In 2008, a seven-year-old girl named Reigh, who lived with her mother in the United Kingdom, was visiting her father, Clark Rockerfeller, who was living in the United States. A social worker was with Reigh to ensure her safety. Reigh's parents had been separated since Reigh was born. Rockerfeller apparently snatched his daughter and took her away on a variety of means of transportation, including yachts. Eventually, Rockerfeller was arrested, and Reigh was returned to her mother.

A child, such as Molly/Misbah (above), whose parents decide to live in different countries, often has to face the additional pressures of different cultures and values.

What about the children?

Sometimes a parent may take their child on vacation to their country of origin, but they don't come back. Sometimes children are "snatched" or abducted and then taken abroad. The other parent may then have to go through lengthy and complicated court proceedings to try and get his or her child returned home.

According to an international agreement called the Hague Convention, children under the age of 16 who are unlawfully taken from the country where they normally live, must be returned to that country. This agreement is signed by over 45 nations, but in practice, it is not always easy to enforce. International custody disputes can be both long and bitter; children are caught, literally, between two countries. In some situations, this may be extremely distressing.

TALK ABOUT

* Do you think mothers are better suited than fathers to being the main carers for children when a relationship breaks down?
* Should both parents have equal rights to their children?

Chapter 7

What challenges does the "new" family face?

Any change within a family, even a happy occasion such as the birth of a new baby, can be unsettling as family members adjust to the changes. When a family first breaks up, young people have to deal with the shock of the situation. Then they have to adjust to everyday life within their new or re-formed family. The impact of the breakup can affect many different aspects of life, from school to other relationships.

Dealing with school

When you're going through a family breakup, school can sometimes seem like a safe place, away from all the upset and arguments at home. At other times, it can seem like another problem—how can you concentrate on schoolwork when your dad or mom has just left home? Exams and choosing subjects can seem like extra problems that you just can't deal with on top of everything else going on in your life.

The feelings children have when their family breaks up don't stay behind at home. Whether the child feels sad or angry, they sometimes let go of their emotions at school by behaving badly. They may mess around in class, bully other children, or be rude to the teachers. This doesn't help them; instead, it often only leads to more problems.

If you are having trouble concentrating at school because of a breakup, try talking to a school counselor. Most schools have counselors to help support pupils having a hard time at home.

Schoolwork

If you are moving to a new house or staying with relatives while things are straightened out at home, it's easy to lose track of schoolwork. Perhaps you have to help take care of the younger children more, or support your parent in other ways, leaving you with less time for homework. Talk about this to a teacher you like and explain the situation. He or she will probably help you find a way to manage your work and keep on top of everything.

Truancy

When parents are preoccupied with the breakdown of a relationship and setting up a new home, perhaps having to work longer hours, some young people think no one at home will notice if they start to miss school. However, the school usually finds out eventually and the child gets into trouble, which only adds to everyone's difficulties.

They just argue

At school events or parents' evenings, do you invite both parents, or choose one? If they both come, will they just argue, or will one refuse to come if the other is there? Try suggesting that they take turns attending events that matter to you, and be firm about no arguments if they attend together!

It can be hard to concentrate at school if your family life is unhappy, but missing school will only cause more problems in the long run.

TALK ABOUT

* Do you think a child's bad behavior at school is excusable if they are experiencing a family breakup?

* Should teachers be more lenient toward children whose parents are splitting up?

Staying in touch

It may not always be easy to see the parent who no longer lives with you. This can be due to bad feelings between the adults, difficulties for the absent parent, or because children feel so hurt by the family breakup that they don't want to see the parent.

Making plans to see a parent can be difficult if there is a lot of bad feeling between the two parents. Sometimes the parent with whom children live may feel so angry and bitter that they try to prevent children from continuing their relationship with the other parent. There may sometimes be another reason for this—perhaps the parent is unsure of the children's safety and wellbeing. Ask your parent to explain the situation, so you understand what's going on and why your parent feels this way.

There are many ways to stay in touch with a parent, even if you are unable to see them.

I'm always let down

Imagine you've been looking forward to seeing your mom or dad all week. Just before he or she is due to pick you up, there's a phone call—suddenly the visit is canceled. This can be very upsetting. It's important to talk about how it makes you feel; although talking won't magically bring your parent to see you, it will help your parents to understand how you feel.

When a parent has left home, it is sometimes hard to pick up the relationship again. At first, things will feel different. It takes time to build a relationship out of a few hours or days a week, when you have been used to spending lots of time together. You may feel angry toward the parent, and let down. The parent may also feel awkward and guilty. Talking and time can help you both to establish a new, happy, and positive relationship.

Two of everything

Shared care means living in two homes. Young people often have two toothbrushes, hairbrushes, and sets of pyjamas. The benefits of this are that parents jointly share the care, and the young person receives love and attention equally from both parents. However, it can take a while to get used to the practical difficulties of moving between two homes.

It takes time and patience to rebuild a relationship with a parent you don't often see.

DOs & DON'Ts

* Do keep in touch with an absent parent by telephone, email, webcam, or letters.

* Don't be surprised if some visits are less successful than others—they can't all be great.

* Don't assume your parent can guess what you like doing on visits—explain what you like best. He or she will probably be relieved to sit and talk rather than try to organize special outings for every visit.

* Do talk to your parent if you know a party is coming up that will interfere with your parent's visit, so that no one is disappointed and other plans can be made.

* Do use a calendar to keep track of where you are staying if you have two homes.

Stressed parents

When both parents live together, they often share the care of their children, such as taking them to friends and activities, preparing food, or supervising bedtimes. When one parent moves out, the sole responsibility falls on the other parent. This can be extremely tiring for that parent and may also be very stressful.

One parent may also have to do more paid work outside the home, to make up for the reduced income. A parent on his or her own may seem more stressed and tired than usual. This can be hard for a young person to accept just when they themselves need additional support. It helps if they try to understand the demands and pressures on the parent.

It's not just children who have to deal with difficult feelings. There are lots of adjustments for parents following a breakup.

It happened to me

"I dreaded birthdays. Who would I spend the day with? I loved getting two sets of presents, but I always felt bad about leaving Mom or leaving Dad if I stayed with Mom. Eventually, I said I wanted to go to my grandma's. That made my parents realize what pressure I felt. Since then, they take turns each year—no discussions."

Sophia, age 11.

Jealousy

Your parents have split up: you go to a friend's house and both their parents are together, or you hear a friend telling you about what he or she did with their mom and dad. It can make you feel jealous and resentful. You might feel angry with your parent that he or she couldn't keep your family together, but each family's situation is different. You cannot know what really goes on in other families. And your own parents may not have told you everything that led to their own relationship breakdown—remember, parents often try to protect their children from difficult or upsetting information.

If a parent remarries, it may be difficult to accept that they have formed a new relationship. Try to remember that just because they have a new partner, it does not mean they love you any less.

No boundaries

Some young people feel that after a parent has left, all boundaries are broken. They feel angry. Why should they obey either parent? They go out, come back late, and behave rudely. Acting in this way won't help anyone. It's more useful to talk openly and calmly to your parents about how you feel, or to other relatives or friends if you don't feel your parents are listening to you or understand how you feel.

Dating game

Parents may also start new relationships, and eventually, they may want to live with their new partner. This can be hard to accept. It can feel embarrassing to see your parent going out on dates and behaving more like a love-struck teenager than a responsible parent. You may not like your parent's new boy or girlfriend. Perhaps you want to spoil any chances he or she has with new relationships. Try to see that this is unfair—everyone has a right to healthy, happy relationships.

Stepfamilies

When a parent meets and sets up home with a new partner, the new partner becomes a stepparent. New partners may often come with children, too! A single-parent family might suddenly grow into a family with a new parent and new brothers and sisters. There is a lot to adjust to, and everyone has to find a way of fitting in. It doesn't happen overnight, and it's not always simple.

New family, new house—it can seem like too much change. But remember, everyone is getting used to the new situation.

DOs & DON'Ts

✳ **Do try to figure out why you don't like the new partner. Perhaps you're angry that he or she has replaced your other parent, or put out that he or she has caused yet more change just when you were getting used to being with only one parent.**

✳ **Do tell another adult if you feel unsafe with the stepparent, or any new partner.**

✳ **Do talk to your parent and stepparent about any difficulties with stepbrothers and sisters. It's normal for brothers and sisters to argue, but it can feel more complex when you're forced into sharing a home with other young people you would not choose to know!**

✳ **Don't expect that bad behavior or rudeness will make your stepparent disappear—it won't.**

New relationships

What happens if a child doesn't get along with the parent's new partner? These feelings are probably manageable if the couple doesn't live together, but there may be problems if they move in with each other. Much younger stepbrothers and sisters often come with a stepparent—much older ones may have left home. It can be hard to suddenly have a toddler around, or an older sister who is allowed to do things that you aren't yet allowed to do. It's a time of adjustment for everyone. You may not ever become best friends with stepsiblings, but life will be a lot easier if you find a way to get along.

It may be that everyone in the new family seems to be happy with the new setup and to find it exciting—except you. No one seems to care what you think. You may feel invisible and left out. It's up to you to explain to the others how you feel, so that they can then help you.

Not all stepmothers are as wicked as the character in the Snow White story! Try to forget the stereotype and see that a stepmother is an ordinary person, just like you.

In the media

From Snow White's wicked stepmother (below) to the negative stereotypes of modern stepparents, stepparents have a bad name. They are often presented as trying to replace the child's biological parent, or as treating their stepchildren less kindly than their own. It's a difficult job for everyone involved. Whereas children and their biological parents have had years to build their relationships with each other, stepparents and children are expected to establish close living relationships in a short time.

The absent parent

A stepparent does not replace your absent biological parent. A stepparent has few legal rights over the children of another relationship, unless he or she adopts the children or takes on parental responsibility in law. The rights of the other parent are not affected.

When one parent falls in love with someone new and sets up home with him or her, the other parent may feel very upset. Although it is distressing to see either parent unhappy, it is important not to get caught up in their feelings. One parent's new relationship should not affect the arrangements made for children to see their other biological parent. If you are worried that a new relationship will make it harder for you to see your other parent, tell your parents about your anxieties and ask them to explain how the existing setup will continue.

Try to see things from your stepparent's viewpoint—they, too, may be finding living in a new family difficult.

It happened to me

"My dad remarried and I went to live with him, his new wife, and her children. For a while, it felt like I was just living in a stranger's house. There were different rules about going out, computer time, bedtime, homework. I was so fed up with it, because the way I'd been allowed to do things changed—the others continued as usual. There was a big argument between me and my dad and stepmom. I think they must have realized it was unfair—now there are new rules for all of us."

Tom, age 12.

TALK ABOUT

✳ Do you think a parent should ask their children's opinion before moving in with another partner?

✳ Do you think parents have the right to start a new relationship?

New people

A change of home, sharing a room with a stepbrother or sister who you really wouldn't choose to be friends with, and seeing your parent meet a new partner is a lot to take in. But it's not just you who has to deal with the change—so, too, do your stepsiblings. They might not want to share a room with you either, and they may not want your parent as their stepparent.

Rather than arguing, try to calmly explain how you feel if you are finding life in a new family hard.

It's common to feel jealous of a parent's new partner or other children in the family. You might think that your parent only cares about the new partner, or seems to favor the stepchildren. But new relationships take time for adults, too. At first, they might not get the balance right in making everyone feel included and special. Talk to your parent, and your stepparent, about your feelings. Ask your parent to spend some time with you, separately from the new partner or siblings.

41

Chapter 8

Moving on

Change can be positive! You didn't want things to change, and things won't go back to the way they were, but people can move on. A family that changes is nothing to be ashamed of and it happens to thousands of people. Any change takes time to get used to. Things will be different, but they can also be good.

Children from famous families face the same difficulties after a relationship breakup.

In the media

Madonna and Guy Ritchie divorced in 2008. This extremely wealthy couple have three children: one biological child, one child from a previous relationship, and one young adopted child. After all the attention has died down and the family members get used to their new living arrangements, the family will be re-formed. Famous or not, every family breakup creates new family formations and new relationships within it.

Time for change

Unhappy parents who live together argue, ignore each other, say mean things, look sad, and are bad-tempered. Once they have separated, they both usually find that things work much better. After a breakup, there is time for everyone to adjust to the new situation. During this time, don't be afraid to ask friends and family for help and support.
If things are difficult at home, or you need a break, spend some time with friends or other family members—but make sure your parent always knows where you are.

A family breakup often brings other family members closer, such as grandparents and grandchildren.

DOs & DON'Ts

It's important to take care of yourself:

✳ **Don't feel guilty about going out with friends and having a good time. Your parents' relationship has changed, but that doesn't mean you have to feel sad all the time. It's OK to have fun and take care of yourself.**

✳ **Do talk to a parent, doctor, or school counselor if you find that your mood remains very down for a long time.**

✳ **Do speak up for yourself. When a family is changing, there are a lot of pressures on everyone. It's easy for children to sink into the background as the adults try to straighten everything out. But it's important that those adults know how you feel.**

✳ **Do ask your parents about their relationship if you are worried about them arguing a lot. You can't change their relationship, but it does no harm for them to know about your anxieties.**

A deeper relationship

Many young people find that they develop better and deeper relationships with their parents after a breakup. They become closer to each parent in different ways. Brother and sister relationships can also become stronger, since there are fewer tensions in the new family setup, and the siblings have supported each other through a difficult period.

Your own relationships

The fact that one couple's relationship didn't last does not mean that your own relationships won't work out. The parent left because the adult relationship broke down—not because of the relationship between parent and child. There is no reason why your own relationships, with friends and boy or girlfriends, will not last.

Don't be afraid of healthy arguments! Just because you argue with a parent or friend, it doesn't follow that the relationship is about to collapse. You may associate arguments with your parents' breakup, but in lots of other relationships, arguments are one method people use to resolve their problems and their issues. They can be helpful and positive as well as negative.

The breakdown of a parents' relationship has an effect on everyone in the family, but young people in the family can continue to develop their own strong and independent relationships.

Support

Grandparents, friends, teachers, and schools counselors—all of these people can be great sources of support for young people experiencing the difficulties of a family breakup. Chatting about your feelings or letting off steam about how unfair it all feels doesn't change the situation, but it does make it feel easier to deal with.

There are also lots of organizations that offer free and confidential advice and support. Check out the list of websites on page 47.

Families are about strong, loving, and caring relationships. A family can take on a new shape, wherever you live and whomever you live with.

TALK ABOUT

* What positive things happen when a family breaks up?
* Do you think it is possible to enjoy a rearranged family without betraying the memory of the old family?
* How can a rearranged family look toward the future?

Glossary

abduct To take a person without permission.

abuse To cause physical or emotional harm to another person.

addiction When someone cannot stop doing something that is bad for them, such as drinking alcohol or taking drugs.

adopt To have permanent legal responsibility for a child or young person.

biological parent Parent who created a child.

child support Money one parent gives to another to help pay for things a child needs.

counselor Someone who you can talk to about your feelings and who is qualified to help you work out your problems.

couple Two people in a relationship.

court A place where a judge hears about issues and conflicts and makes decisions about them.

custody To have responsibility for taking care of a child the majority of the time. A child lives with the parent who has custody.

disagreement When people cannot agree on a particular subject.

divorce The legal ending to a marriage.

foster When a couple temporarily looks after and takes on responsibility for someone else's child.

homosexual relationship Sexual relationship between two women or two men.

issues Emotional problems or difficulties.

legal agreement A document that is accepted by a court of law.

mediation Professional support for couples who are splitting up, to help them do so with as little conflict as possible.

nurture To care for someone or something.

prejudice To have negative thoughts about someone based on their background.

preoccupied When someone is absorbed in their own thoughts and can seem distant as a result.

reassurance Telling someone everything will be OK.

separation When a couple splits up.

sibling A brother or sister.

social worker A person who is trained to help support individuals and families.

stereotype Labeling someone as a particular type of person because of their background, class, social situation, or other type of category.

Further Information and Web Sites

Notes for Teachers:

The Talk About panels are to be used to encourage debate and avoid the polarization of views. One way of doing this is to use "continuum lines." Think of a range of statements or opinions about the topics that can then be considered by the pupils. An imaginary line is constructed that pupils can stand along to show what they feel in response to each statement (please see above). If they strongly agree or disagree with the viewpoint, they can stand by the signs, if the response is somewhere in between, they stand along the line in the relevant place. If the response is "neither agree, nor disagree" or they "don't know," then they stand at an equal distance from each sign, in the middle. Alternatively, continuum lines can be drawn on paper and pupils can mark a cross on the line to reflect their views.

Books to read

Know the Facts About Relationships
Sarah Medina
(Rosen Central, 2009)

The Bright Side: Surviving Your Parents Divorce
Max Sindell
(HCI, 2007)

When Parents Separate
Pete Sanders
(Stargazer Books, 2006)

Web Sites

Due to the changing nature of Internet links, Rosen Publishing has developed an online list of Web sites related to the subject of this book. This site is regularly updated. Please use this link to access this list:
http://www.rosenlinks.com/act/fami

Index

Entries in **bold** are for pictures.